MW01170900

SELF
REGULATION

FOR KIDS 8-12

ENGAGING CBT ACTIVITIES AND GAMES TO HELP KIDS COPE WITH ANGER, STRESS AND OTHER STRONG EMOTIONS

BY

JESSY TORPHY

Table of Contents

Note to Parents & Kids!

Welcome to "Self-Regulation for Kids 8-12!" This book is designed to help children develop essential skills to manage their emotions, thoughts, and behaviors. Through fun CBT activities, games, and exercises, kids will learn how to recognize their feelings, practice calming techniques, and make positive choices.

Throughout the book, parents will find tips and suggestions to support their child's journey. These activities can strengthen your parent-child bond and enhance your learning experience.

Thoughts, Feelings, Behaviors, and Self-Regulation

Emotional dysregulation, sometimes known as dysregulation, is the inability to manage or regulate one's emotional reactions. This can cause major mood swings or emotional instability. Many emotions and feelings can be involved, including annoyance, irritability, grief, and anger.

Generally speaking, emotional dysregulation is the state of having too strong emotions for one's current situation. This can involve ignoring tough emotions, being unable to cool off, or emphasizing the negative events in your life. You may act impulsively when your emotions (fear, sadness, or anger) are extremely strong.

These issues often start at a young age and can spiral into self-regulation problems if not treated early; this is why this book, "Self-regulation for Kids" will significantly aid children! Starting early is the best solution to correcting emotional dysregulation issues, and the activities and games given in this book will make the experience fun for kids!

Identifying and Understanding the Feelings

Emotional dysregulation can affect kids in many ways, which causes them to lash out in ways you may not understand; however, some common signs can indicate that your child may need help self-regulating:

- Having trouble regulating their moods

- Easily frustrated by small inconveniences

- Mood swings

- Impulsive behavior

- Losing their temper easily

- Constant irritable behavior

SIGNS OF EMOTIONAL DYSREGULATION

Overly Intense
Emotions

Impulsive
Behavior

Lack of Emotional
Awareness

Trouble Making
Decisions

Inability to Manage
Behavior

Avoids Difficult
Emotions

It may seem strange and daunting when these changes in mood occur. This book uses Cognitive Behavioral Therapy (CBT) approaches to help you recognize and understand emotions. CBT helps you to see how your thoughts, emotions, and actions are all connected. Understanding your emotions will help you to better see how you can shape your behavior. Every chapter offers enjoyable exercises meant to help you develop these abilities, including coloring your emotions or a daily feelings journal. CBT activities help you replace your negative thoughts and emotions with the positive ones, allowing yourself to control your feelings. We will create your self-regulation and emotional well-being toolkit together!

How to Use this Book!

Hey there! I'm excited for you to finally start this self-regulation book! Before you begin, let me introduce you to Stephanie, a young girl who will help you in your self-regulation journey through all the practices and activities given in the book! Here are some tips to help you get started:

Read Together: Read the introduction with your parents and learn why self-regulation is important.

Try the Activities: Each section has fun activities designed to help you practice self-regulation, involve the family in these exercises, and learn to develop self-regulation together!

Take It Slow: No need to rush! You can take your time with each activity.

Talk It Out: After each activity, discuss with your parents what you have learned. Tell them how you felt and what strategies worked for you.

What am I Feeling?

Hello kids! My name is Stephanie! I'm 10 years old and have to face big emotions, just like you! My mom and dad often help me manage these big emotions. They have taught me many methods to stay calm when I feel these big emotions. They have even gotten me a service dog, Max, to help me calm down when they are not with me!

You may also experience big emotions like I do at times, and I completely understand how confusing and frustrating it can be when you can't understand why you always react in big ways. This is why I'm here to help you through all the confusing and difficult emotions you experience, and develop self-regulation skills!

Activity 1

MY EMOTIONS WHEEL

I am here to help and guide you through the journey of learning to recognize and control your emotions! Regulating emotions through different activities was a cool idea my mom and dad taught me! It was a bit difficult for me at first as I could never stay calm long enough to work through the activity, but my parents guided me patiently, and I was able to practice these activities without showing any big emotions!

Whenever I felt frustrated, I didn't know why I was so restless, but with the help of this emotions wheel, I could feel what emotions upset me, and I could deal with them without causing my mom and dad any worry! You can do the same by solving the given activity.

The first step in learning to calm down is recognizing which emotions upset you. This emotions wheel can help you! Take a look at the given emotions. Can you recognize which emotions you feel when you're frustrated, sad, happy, etc.? Color in the emotions! For me, the angry emotion feels like a red color, but it may feel like a purple or orange color for you! So, color the emotions in the wheel and talk about a time you felt these emotions with your mom and dad.

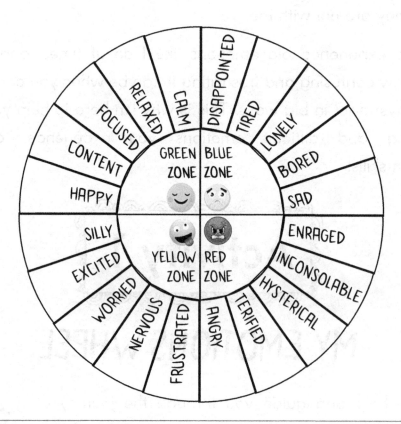

Activity 2

MY MOOD METER

Hi friends! It's good to see you again! How did you like going through the previous activity? I bet you have learned a lot of new things about your inner emotions! The following activity will also help you do the same.

The Mood Meter is one of my favorite exercises because it helps me recognize my feelings when I'm frustrated. Here is what you will need to do. The mood meter is made up of 4 colors: Green, Red, Yellow, and Blue. You can even color the emotions!

All of these colors have energy levels:

Yellow: High energy feelings (comfortable feelings)

Joyful   Hopeful

Focused   Happy

Blue: Low energy feelings (uncomfortable feelings)

Sad   Miserable

Hopeless   Bored

Exhausted

Green: Low energy feelings (comfortable feelings)

Calm   Grateful

Loving   Thoughtful

Balanced

Red: High energy feelings (uncomfortable feelings)

Frightened   Worried

Annoyed   Angry

Here is what you will need to do if you start to feel your emotions getting too overwhelming:

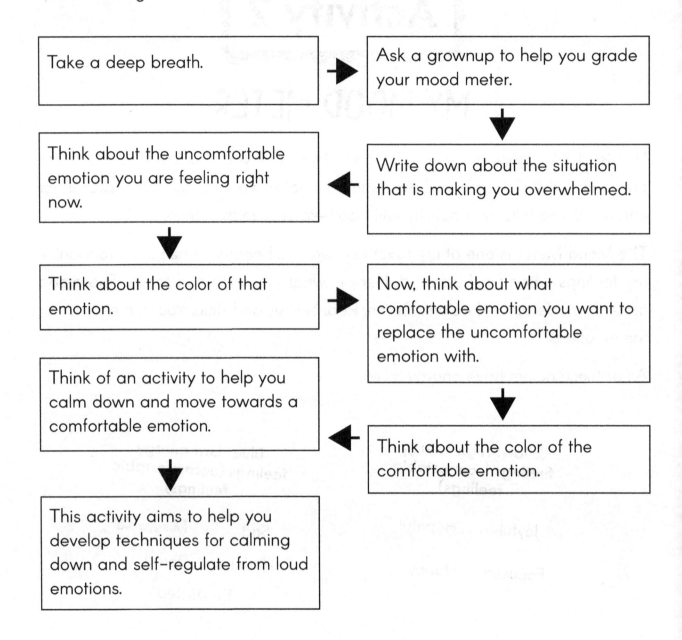

Take a deep breath.

Ask a grownup to help you grade your mood meter.

Think about the uncomfortable emotion you are feeling right now.

Write down about the situation that is making you overwhelmed.

Think about the color of that emotion.

Now, think about what comfortable emotion you want to replace the uncomfortable emotion with.

Think of an activity to help you calm down and move towards a comfortable emotion.

Think about the color of the comfortable emotion.

This activity aims to help you develop techniques for calming down and self-regulate from loud emotions.

The next step is to color in your emotions! Coloring is always the best part of this activity for me because I love to color! Coloring in shades of my emotions is always helpful in recognizing how much or how little of a certain emotion I'm feeling. For instance, when you feel a little sad, it can be a soft powder blue, but when you feel very sad, it can be a dark navy blue.

Let me give you an example: a few weeks ago, I was looking forward to eating ice cream after dinner, but my mom said I couldn't have ice cream because I had already had a snack earlier in the day. I felt annoyed, but it was a light, pastel red. Then, a few days later, my dog Max ate my homework! I had to stay up late and do it all over again. I was really, really annoyed, and this time, the shade of red was carmine.

But both times, I could calm down with the help of the mood meter. You can also use the same method and give your emotions different shades! This can help you realize the degree to which you feel an emotion, and you can self-regulate easily!

You can use the given image for this, so go ahead and color in all the emotions!

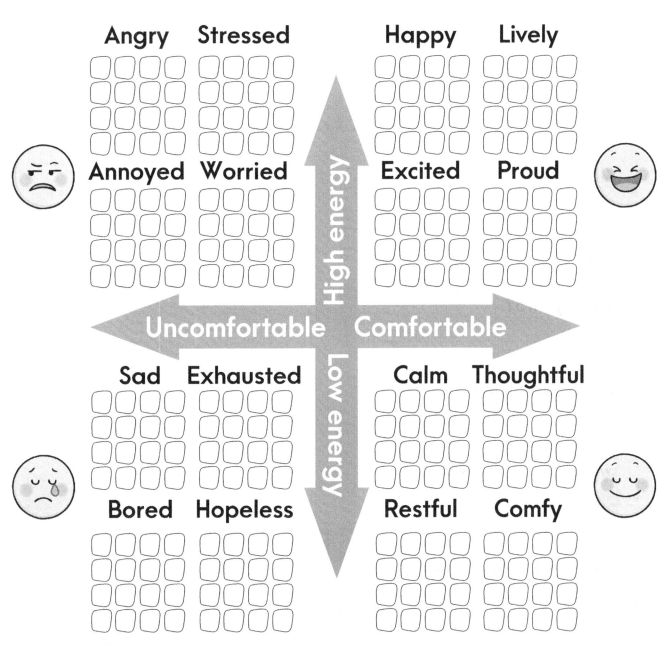

Now that you have learned how the mood meter works, let's practice! I will give you an imaginary situation, and you can use this exercise to see how the situation makes you feel, what color it is, which emotion and color you want to change it into, and what practice/technique you can use to self-regulate.

Scenario 1: Someone at school stole your favorite pen.

What uncomfortable feeling am I having?	
What color is it?	
What shade is it?	
Which comfortable feeling do I want to change this feeling into?	
What color is it?	
What shade is it?	
What can I do to make this change?	

14

Scenario 2: You heard your best friend gossiping about you.

What uncomfortable feeling am I having?

What color is it?

What shade is it?

Which comfortable feeling do I want to change this feeling into?

What color is it?

What shade is it?

What can I do to make this change?

Scenario 3: Your mom won't buy you the toy you want.

What uncomfortable feeling am I having?	
What color is it?	
What shade is it?	
Which comfortable feeling do I want to change this feeling into?	
What color is it?	
What shade is it?	
What can I do to make this change?	

Scenario 4: You really want to see your favorite movie, but all the tickets are sold out when you arrive at the theatre.

What uncomfortable feeling am I having?	
What color is it?	
What shade is it?	
Which comfortable feeling do I want to change this feeling into?	
What color is it?	
What shade is it?	
What can I do to make this change?	

Scenario 5: Your dad promised to take you shopping but cannot take time off for the shopping trip due to a work emergency.

What uncomfortable feeling am I having?	
What color is it?	
What shade is it?	
Which comfortable feeling do I want to change this feeling into?	
What color is it?	
What shade is it?	
What can I do to make this change?	

Note to Parents

You can sit with your child and help them color in the intensity of their emotions. The different shades associated with emotions can help them recognize to what degree they are feeling an overwhelming emotion, if it is okay for them to feel this emotion to this degree, and if they should tone down feeling so worked up over a small matter.

Activity 3

SELF-REGULATION SCENARIO CARDS

When I do my self-regulation exercises that can help me calm my emotions, I always like to mix in a little bit of fun! I love playing games, and self-regulation activities can get a bit boring, so my mom taught me this cool game that I can play to calm down.

It's called Scenario Cards, and whenever I feel angry, I take it out and spin the wheel to land on a scenario that I can use to distract myself from my big and uncomfortable emotions.

Let's play together! You can cut out and assemble the given wheels. Spin the wheel whenever you need an alternate scenario for your big emotions! By practicing the alternate scenarios, you can distract yourself from your current emotions and learn to self-regulate better!

Top Wheel

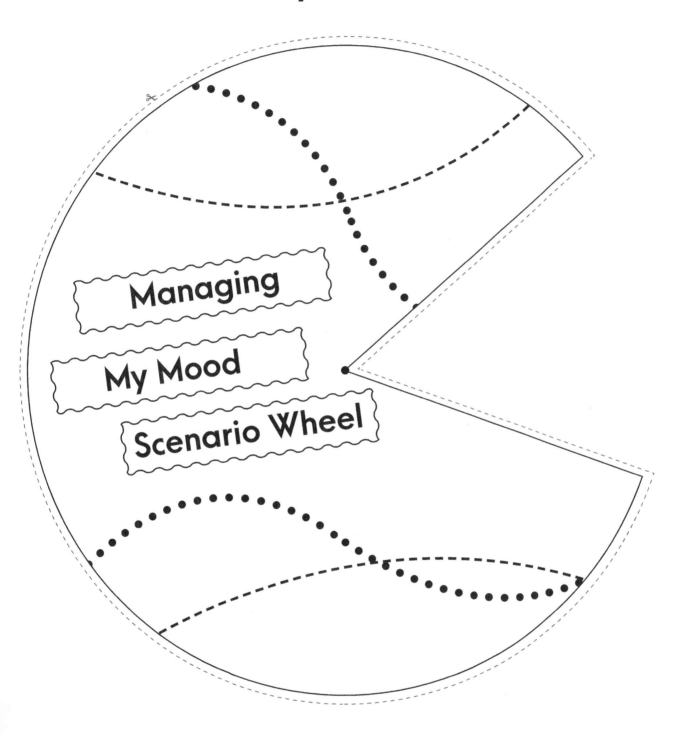

Managing

My Mood

Scenario Wheel

Bottom Wheel

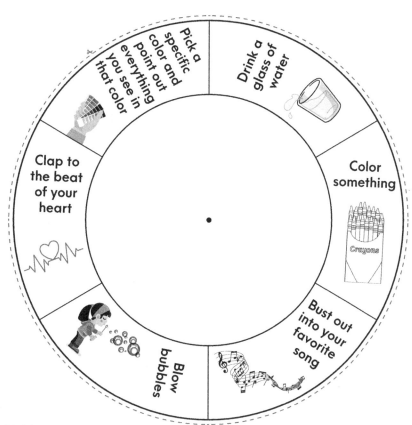

Middle Wheel

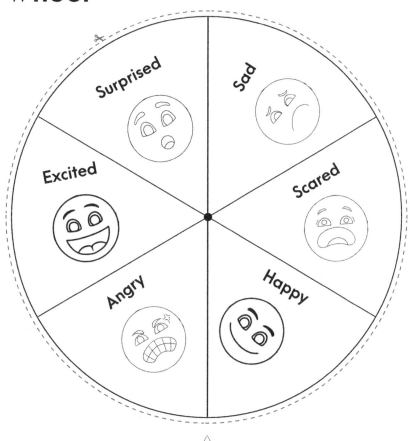

13

Instructions:

1. Color the given wheels.
2. Cut out all three wheels and place them in their appropriate spot: top, middle, and bottom.
3. Attach them in the middle using a pin or a fastener.
4. Spin the wheel when you need to calm down and enjoy the fun activities!

Note to Parents

Play this game with your child, perform the calm-down scenarios, and direct their attention towards the changing of their emotions from hyper to calm. Help them recognize the change and the state or feeling of both extremes (hyper and calm) in their body. Gently direct them towards the relaxing effect of calmness and the toll hyper emotions take on their body.

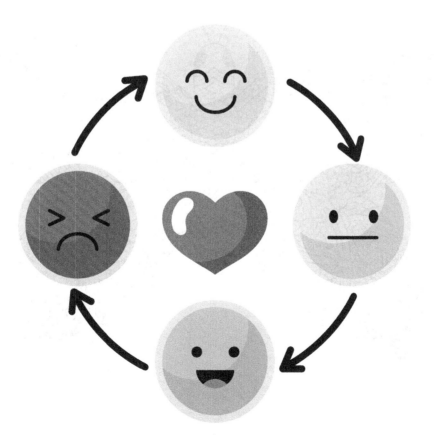

Activity 4

CALMING COLORING PAGES

After the fun game we played in the last activity, my favorite wind down is coloring! My dream is to be an artist when I grow up, so it's even more fun when I can combine my self-regulation activities with my favorite hobby and future career!

Coloring can be a very effective strategy for self-regulation. For me personally, it helps to mute out all the disturbing emotions and hyper-feelings in my head, and I can calmly focus on the colors on the page and my breathing! Being aware of my breathing is an effective way to self-regulate faster!

Color My Calm, Blue!

Color these images in shades of blue, and think about the emotions you associate with blue color.

Color My Calm, Green!

Color these images in shades of green, and think about the emotions you associate with green color.

Color My Calm, Yellow!

Color these images in shades of yellow, and think about the emotions you associate with yellow color.

Color My Calm, Red!

Color these images in shades of red, and think about the emotions you associate with red color.

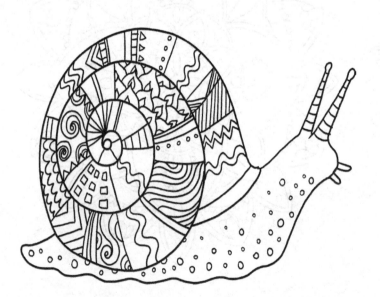

Color My Calm, Purple!

Color these images in shades of purple, and think about the emotions you associate with purple color.

Color My Calm, Pink!

Color these images in shades of pink, and think about the emotions you associate with pink color.

Color My Calm, Brown!

Color these images in shades of brown, and think about the emotions you associate with brown color.

Note to Parents

Color the activity pages with your child. Talk to them about the colors you associate with different emotions, if your child feels the same way or if the link between color and feeling is different for both of you.

MY FEELINGS THERMOMETER

Friends! You must feel refreshed after coloring your emotions. Coloring is a relaxing activity, and it always helps me feel calm and better!

Let me show you another activity that helps me feel better when I get big, uncomfortable emotions. It's called a 'Feelings Thermometer' I used to get agitated really fast, and it was hard for me to control and calm myself down because I could not tell the signs that I was getting upset and overwhelmed.

One day, when I had a big tantrum, my dad sat me down and explained to me that it was not good for my health to feel so many and such intense emotions in such a short time. I explained to my dad that I could never tell when I was feeling overwhelmed, so I couldn't calm myself down before exploding.

Then my dad told me something incredible! There actually were some signs that I could be on the lookout for to self-regulate my emotions before they got out of control! Did you know that when someone gets angry, their breath flares up, and their face gets red? I had never realized this before my dad told me this! With the help of my dad's advice, I could recognize the other signs my body was giving me all along, but I was unable to recognize them until that point! This was very helpful, and I started to self-regulate better by recognizing these signs!

You can also recognize the changes in your body and mental state; this will help you calm down faster than ever before! Use these signs as a thermometer to determine when your body starts to tell you that you are feeling big emotions and when the thermometer reaches a fever pitch, i.e., you need to step away and calm down. You can also color the given pictures!

When I Am in the Red Area, My Body Feels:

Red Area:

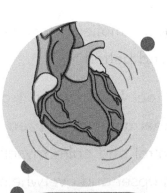

My heart beats faster

My body becomes stiff

My hands are clenched

I feel hot

I am breathing hard and shallow

32

Yellow Area:

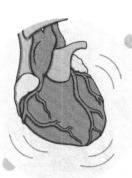

My heart beats faster

I have loud thoughts and feelings

My body feels wriggly

My hands feel sweaty

My breathing is faster

When I Am in the Green Area, My Body Feels:

Green Area

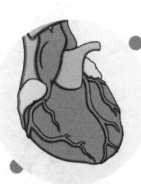

My heart is calm

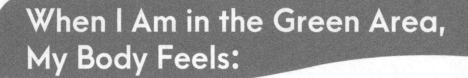

My body is relaxed

I feel at peace

I can focus and learn properly

My breathing is slow and deep

Blue Area

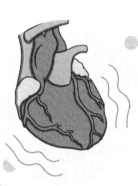

My heart
feels heavy

My body
feels tired

I have no energy

I can't think clearly

I want to rest

Note to Parents

Sit with your child and help them recognize the signs in their body. Relate these to an incident they might have had in the past regarding their emotions flaring up. Talk them through calm-down methods if they start to feel fussy, overwhelmed, and have trouble regulating their emotions.

Activity 6

ROLE-PLAY GAMES

Role-play games are one of my favorite calm-down activities. It's fun to listen to the stories and imagine my response in the same situation! Let me tell you how it will work!

First, you will read a story, then imagine yourself in the character's shoes and try to see what behaviors they showed in the story were big, uncomfortable emotions. You will also write down any methods that they could have used instead to calm themselves down. This is a fun way to incorporate role-playing games into your self-regulation practices!

Role-Play Story 1:

Amy is excited to start the 5th grade. She is a straight-A student and can't wait to start the new school year and learn new things! Soon, her classes begin, and she strives towards a straight A final grade again. However, Amy is a bit disheartened when she realizes that the 5th grade is tougher than she thought. She becomes agitated and often gets rude to her friends and family due to the pressure of performing well in school, but all this only adds to Amy's stress instead of lessening it. Finally, it reaches a breathing point when Amy gets a C instead of an A on her math test. She throws a tantrum when she gets home and breaks down crying. Her mother tries to calm her down, but Amy feels too emotional to listen to anyone. Finally, after hours of crying, Amy calms down and tells her mother what happened. Her mother reassures her and talks her through the difficult emotions Amy still feels. Together, they are able to figure everything out and form a strategy that can help Amy calm down the next time she starts to feel big emotions.

Time Out

From the story, you can see that Amy was frustrated at being unable to keep up with her studies, resulting in a tantrum. However, there were signs that Amy was getting frustrated. After reading the story, can you suggest a few methods Amy could have used to calm down? What would you have done if you were in Amy's place?

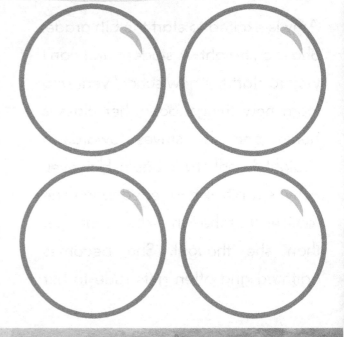

Role-Play Story 2:

Emily is a 10-year-old girl who is very excited to go shopping with her mom today. Her birthday is next week, and her mom is going to buy her a dress to wear on her birthday party. Emily has a specific dress in mind, and as soon as they enter the store, she sees the dress hanging on one of the mannequins. Emily is happy that she has found her dream dress so quickly, but there's a problem: it's too expensive! Emily's mom asks her to pick another dress, but Emily is set on getting the expensive one.

Emily starts to get fussy and agitated. In fact, when her mother reprimands her for acting rudely, Emily throws a screaming tantrum in the store! She does not get calm even after coming home, and Emily's

mother has to ask her dad for help. Together, they help Emily calm down and talk about the incident at the store. Emily realizes that what she did was wrong and very rude.

She asks her parents for help, and they devise a few breathing techniques that can help calm down Emily's anger the next time she becomes upset.

Time Out

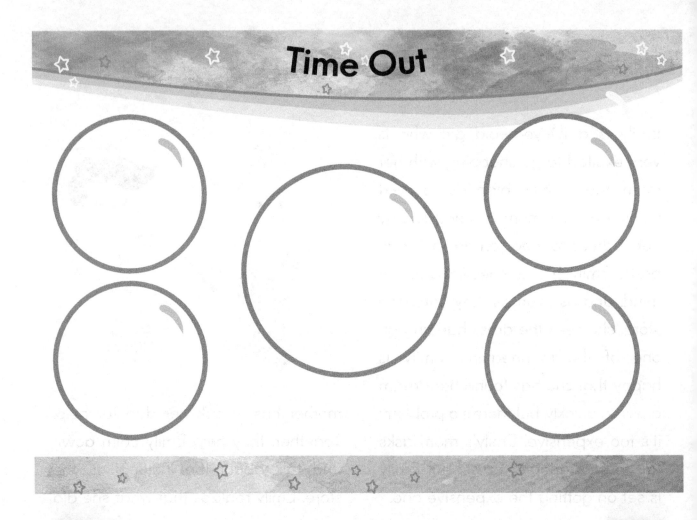

Note to Parents

Sit with your child and present a scenario from their past behavior incidents. Present them with two options:

Option 1: The behavior they exhibited in the past in that situation

Option 2: The opposite choice

Encourage them to choose the positive response in that situation and talk about the intensity of their emotions; this can help children realize that they may have overreacted to a minor inconvenience and make them realize that they can avoid it next time by regulating their emotions correctly.

Activity 7

A OR B?

Hi friends! It's Stephanie again! It's good to see you after so long! I hope you're making some good progress on your self-regulation journey! All the techniques that helped me self-regulate are here, so I hope you're taking full advantage of them!

This exercise focuses on choices. It's easy to learn to regulate emotions when you know that you can make choices to avoid the worst outcome! Take a look at the given scenarios and make your choices!

Scenario 1:

Eli and Jacob are having an argument. Eli doesn't want to play with Jacob because Jacob always gets angry and starts throwing toys when he loses. Jacob promises Eli that it won't happen this time because he has been practicing to control his emotions. However, the same thing happens when Eli wins the game, and Jacob starts to get upset.

If you were in Jacob's place, would you:

A: Start getting upset and angry?

Or

B: Take a few deep breaths to calm yourself down and resume the game?

Scenario 2:

John and Mark are playing netball at school. Mark accidentally drops the ball, which causes their team to lose a point and the match as well. John gets upset with Mark, blaming him for their team's loss. Mark keeps insisting that it was an accident and that he didn't do it on purpose.

If you were in John's place, would you:

A: Take a breath to calm down, bring your heartbeat back to normal, and apologize to Mark for blaming him for the lost game?

Or

B: Keep insisting that he was the reason the team lost the game and unnecessarily get upset with him?

Scenario 3:

Alex and Claire are getting ready to go to a friend's house. Claire is putting on makeup, while Alex chooses not to put on any makeup. Claire gets upset with Alex and tells her that everyone will think she is ugly. Alex feels hurt by this comment and asks Claire to apologize for saying something so rude. If you were Claire, would you:

A: Take a moment to calm down and apologize to Alex for making such a hurtful comment?

Or

B: Double down, stand your ground, and insist you are right?

Note to Parents

Sit with your child and present similar options to them. Encourage them to make a good choice and talk to them about why it is the better choice.

Activity 8

BEFORE I POP

Dear Friends! The last activity in this section is one of my favorites! My dad always helps me go through these activities until I feel calm again. It is a list of things I try when my body starts to feel big, uncomfortable emotions. They help me calm down again, and you can use some of the same techniques or create your own to try before you pop.

 I can try these methods before I POP:

TAKE DEEP BREATHS AND DEVELOP A BREATHING ROUTINE.	WRITE ABOUT YOUR FEELINGS IN A JOURNAL.	DRAW SOMETHING.
HAVE A GLASS OF WATER OR A LIGHT SNACK.	TALK ABOUT IT WITH SOMEONE.	TAKE A SHORT WALK TO CALM DOWN.

Note to Parents

Sit with your child and brainstorm more self-regulation methods that can help them calm down in different situations. Tell them about some techniques you use to calm down when you feel big emotions.

MY SELF-REFLECTION JOURNAL

Hello! It's me again, Stephanie! Did the "My Emotions Wheel" activity at the beginning of this section help you recognize your emotions? I bet it did! It's a really effective activity, and I still use it with the help of my parents whenever I start to feel big emotions again!

These days, I don't get angry so easily, but there was a time when I was upset all the time. Let me tell you a story about the time I was ready for an outburst.

Storytime!

One day, I went to my best friend Lucy's house to play. We were going to spend the whole day playing video games, and I was really excited! You see, Lucy is good at video games, so when she kept beating me, I got really, really angry. I never wanted to talk to Lucy again! But Lucy's mom immediately understood what I was going through. She took me aside and helped me to breathe and calm down. That night, my mom gave me a journal before bedtime. Lucy's mom had talked to her and given her this journal for me! She said that it was something that could help me feel better, and she was right! My feelings improved as I began to write in the journal and express what I was feeling inside in written form.

This is why I truly recommend you to practice this activity, too! A self-reflection journal can help you see the things that cause you to act out, and you can work on building mental strength to control all the emotions you struggle with. Use the given pages to write out all the feelings that bother you!

Over the next 30 days, go through all the prompts and write about your feelings in the feelings journal:

Day 1

Describe a time when you felt happy. What was the occasion, and how did you identify the emotion?

Day 2

Describe a time when you felt angry. What was the occasion, and how did you identify the emotion?

Day 3

What strategies did you use to calm down when you were feeling angry?

Day 4

Name 2 things you are good at. How does this make you feel?

Day 5

Is there anything at home or school that you find challenging? How do you handle this challenge?

Day 6

Imagine this: Your friend has lost their favorite toy, and they are really upset. How would you comfort them?

Day 7

Can you think of a time when you helped someone? How did that make you feel?

Day 8

Are there some qualities or habits that you think you should improve on? What are they? Why do you think you should improve them?

Day 9

Think about a time when you had to reflect on a mistake you made. How did you know it was a mistake, and how did you reflect on your behavior?

Day 10

If you could do anything tomorrow that makes you happy, what would it be?

Day 11

Imagine this: You come back from lunch break at school and find that someone has taken your favorite pen; how do you think you should react to this?

Day 12

Name three people that make you feel loved. What do they do that makes you feel this way?

Day 13

Now, name one thing or habit about each of these three people that upsets or irritates you.

Day 14

List three habits about you that these three people may find irritating.

Day 15

Here's food for thought: Think about these small habits about you that often irritate others and habits in others that often irritate you.

Has there ever been an instance where you felt genuinely upset or hateful towards these people for these irritating habits? Do you think they also genuinely feel irritated by you for your intense emotions?

Day 16

Name a memory from your childhood that makes you happy. Why does it make you smile?

Day 17

What do you usually do when you're feeling down or sad?

Day 18

Take a moment to think about what happens when you feel sad. How do these feelings impact your life?

Day 19

Describe a time when you felt excited about something, but it didn't go as planned. How did this make you feel?

Day 20

Name the thing about any three people who have made you feel better in sad times. What qualities of happiness and comfort do they bring into your life?

Day 21

Name a time in your life when you were really sad and worried about something, but the result turned out okay, for example, an exam you were worried about passing but got a really good grade.

Day 22

Imagine this: You have been waiting all day to watch the airing of your favorite TV show, but your younger sibling wants to watch another one at the same time. Your mom sides with your sibling, and you cannot watch your show. What emotion does this arouse in you? Then, name three things that can distract you from reacting to this emotion.

Day 23

Explain what the emotion of anger feels like in your own words. What does it look like? How does it feel like? How does it feel to the touch? What color is it?

Day 24

List three things that can calm your anger when you start to feel yourself flare up.

Day 25

Here's food for thought: What does it mean to cope with pain? Why do you think having such a quality is important?

Day 26

Write about something that makes you scared or any fear or phobia you may have. What are three methods that you can use to cope with these fears?

Day 27

Imagine this: You see your best friend after a long time. You have been lonely without them and want to spend quality time with them. They organize a sleepover at their house but have to cancel at the last minute due to a family emergency. How does this make you feel? Is it a good feeling or a bad feeling?

Day 28

Describe a time that made you feel anxious and nervous. What was happening around you that made you feel this way? Was there a strategy you could use to make yourself feel calm again at that time?

Day 29

Are there any strategies or techniques that you use to feel less anxious? Name them.

Day 30

If you could say thank you to someone, who would it be and why? What feelings do you experience after saying thank you? Are they good or bad feelings?

Day 1

_____

_____

_____

Day 2

_____

_____

_____

Day 3

_____

_____

_____

Day 4

_____

_____

_____

Day 5

_____

_____

_____

Day 6

_____

_____

_____

Day 7

_____

_____

_____

Day 8

_____

_____

_____

Day 9

_____

_____

_____

Day 10

_____

_____

_____

Day 11

_____

_____

_____

Day 12

_____

_____

_____

Day 13

_____

_____

_____

Day 14

_____

_____

_____

Day 15

_____

_____

_____

Day 16

_____

_____

Day 17

_____

_____

Day 18

_____

_____

Day 19

_____

_____

Day 20

_____

_____

Day 21

_____

_____

Day 22

_____

_____

Day 23

_____

_____

Day 24

_____

_____

Day 25

_____

_____

_____

Day 26

_____

_____

_____

Day 27

_____

_____

_____

Day 28

_____

_____

_____

Day 29

_____

_____

_____

Day 30

_____

_____

_____

Note to Parents

Children often have difficulty realizing that their rude behavior and flared-up emotions can hurt people's feelings. Take some time to sit with them and explain how their responses or impulsive emotions may have hurt the feelings of the people around them.

Activity 10

MY COPING SKILLS CHECKLIST

Some days, I prefer to take a break from all the self-regulation activities. You heard me right, friends! Even I get lazy sometimes.

Writing in my self-regulation book is effective, but I turn to my coping skills checklist when I don't feel like writing anymore!

It's a list that my best friend Lucy and I created together! Whenever I feel frustrated and don't want to do any writing activities, Lucy and I meet up and do a few things on my coping skills checklist!

It helps calm my uncomfortable and big emotions, and I can easily self-regulate without feeling overwhelmed! I'll let you borrow my coping skills checklist; it can help you calm down and control your emotions!

TAKE A BATH

LIGHT A CANDLE

LEARN
SOMETHING NEW

REST YOUR LEGS
UP ON THE WALL

READ A BOOK

TAKE A NAP

WATCH
THE STARS

LISTEN TO MUSIC

TAKE DEEP
BELLY BREATHS

MEANDER
AROUND TOWN

PET A
FURRY ANIMAL

TAKE A
TEA BREAK

WATCH
THE CLOUDS

SIT IN
NATURE

RELAX NEAR A
BODY OF WATER

CALL A FRIEND

LET OUT
A DEEP SIGH

FLY A KITE

77 WAYS
TO TAKE A
BREAK

MOVE TWICE
AS SLOWLY

WRITE A LETTER

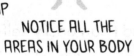
GO TO A FARMER'S
MARKET WITH A
GROWN UP

MOVE TWICE
AS SLOWLY

FIND A
RELAXING SCENT

NOTICE ALL THE
AREAS IN YOUR BODY

EXAMINE AN
EVERYDAY
OBJECTS WITH
FRESH EYES

BUY SOME
FLOWERS

GO SOMEWHERE
NEW

WALK OUTSIDE

GO FOR
A RUN

TURN OFF ALL
ELECTRONICS

TAKE A
BIKE RIDE

GO TO A PARK

EAT A MEAL
IN SILENCE

READ OR
WATCH
SOMETHING
FUNNY

COLOR WITH
CRAYONS

CLIMB A TREE

MAKE SOME
NEW MUSIC WITH
HOUSEHOLD ITEMS
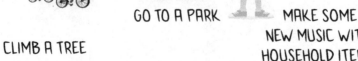

FORGIVE SOMEONE
MEAN TO YOU

SCRUNCH
YOUR EYES

ENGAGE IN A
SMALL ACT
OF KINDNESS

CLEAN SOMETHING

TRY AROMATHERAPHY

PUT ON SOME
MUSIC AND DANCE

KNIT OR SEW

PUNCH A PILLOW

PAINT YOUR NAILS

MEDITATE

DO SOME
STRETCHES

WRITE A POEM

READ POETRY

TEACH YOUR PET
A NEW TRICK

REARRANGE
YOUR ROOM

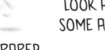
LOOK AT
SOME ART

PAINT ON A
SURFACE THINNER
THAN PAPER

SING

PLAY A MUSICAL
INSTRUMNT

PLAY THE 15
MINUTE GAME

RIP PAPER
INTO TINY PIECES

BAKE COOKIES
WITH A GROWN UP

PUT ON
FAKE TATTOOS

THANK
YOU!

TELL SOMEONE
YOU ARE THANKFUL
TO HAVE THEM
IN YOUR LIFE

DOODLE ON
A PAPER

Crossword puzzle

DO A WORD SEARCH
OR CROSSWORD PUZZLE

LOOK THROUGH
OLD FAMILY ALBUMS

HUG A
STUFFED
ANIMAL

GIVE YOURSELF
A FACIAL

JUMP ON A
TRAMPOLINE

FEED THE
SQUIRRELS OR
BIRDS IN
YOUR GARDEN

COLOR-COORDINATE
YOUR CLOTHES

FACE PAINT

PLAN YOUR
DREAM ROOM
[WITH PAINT,
COLORS, FURNITURE]

WRITE IN
A JOURNAL

Note to Parents

Go through the checklist with your child to see what activities they can do alone and which activities they need help with. You can do some activities with them and leave them to practice the rest independently.

Coping with Intense Emotions

Hi friends, handling intense emotions can be complicated and scary. The first time I had a meltdown, I was exhausted and overwhelmed afterward. It took me a few days to fully be my old self again. My mom and dad also helped me through this process. I apologized to my parents for causing them so much trouble, but they weren't angry! In fact, we sat for a long time and talked about my feelings, what had caused my meltdown, and how I could avoid it the next time I feel big emotions.

BIG PROBLEMS VS. SMALL PROBLEMS

Not all problems are the same, and personally, I have the most trouble judging when a problem is too big or too small. This helps me self-regulate much faster and easier. You can also use the given activity to separate your big and small problems!

Big Problems

What is the problem?

What is the problem?

Medium Problems

What is the problem?

What is the problem?

Small Problem

What is the problem?

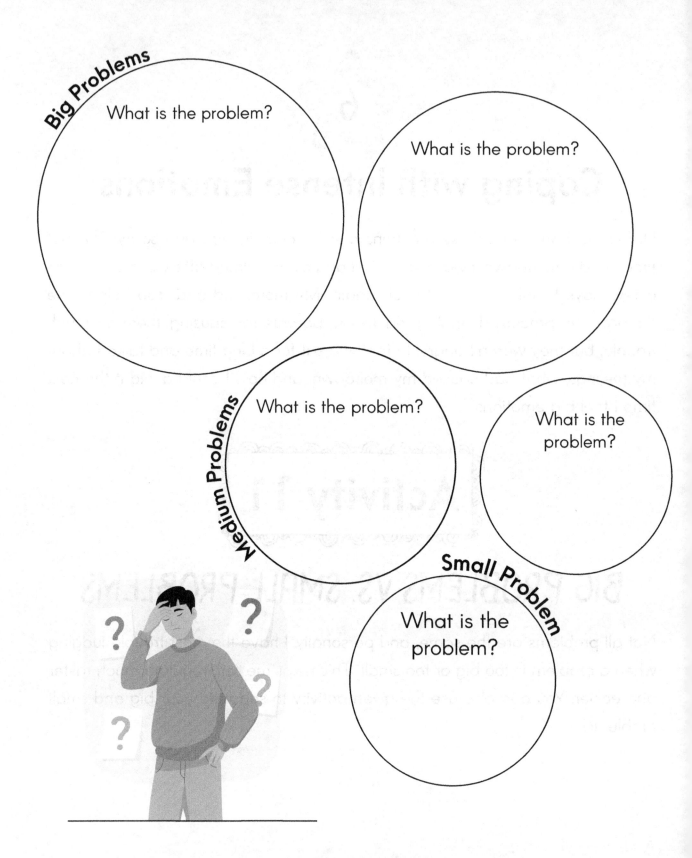

Activity 12

MY MELTDOWN STRATEGIES

Hi Friends! My mom and dad helped me make a list of meltdown strategies that I could use to calm down and talk about my emotions when I was starting to feel frustrated, irritated, or sad. You can also use these strategies to take a break from tiring feelings when they start to feel like too much.

De-Escalation
Strategies for Meltdowns

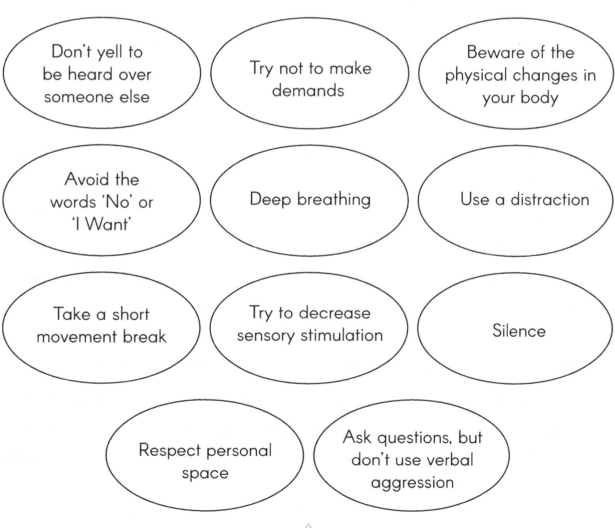

Don't yell to be heard over someone else

Try not to make demands

Beware of the physical changes in your body

Avoid the words 'No' or 'I Want'

Deep breathing

Use a distraction

Take a short movement break

Try to decrease sensory stimulation

Silence

Respect personal space

Ask questions, but don't use verbal aggression

Activity 13

MY COPING PINWHEEL

Friends! The Coping Pinwheel is a fun activity I learned from my science teacher at school. There is an interesting story behind the incident; one day, we learned about space and the planets in class. My friend Andrew asked the teacher if aliens were real. Friends, let me tell you this: I believe in aliens! When the teacher told Andrew that aliens might exist, but no one had confirmed it yet, I began to feel sad and depressed. I could barely focus on the lesson, and I kept getting more depressed. After a while, our teacher noticed my silent behavior and asked me what was wrong.

I told him everything because my parents had been practicing with me to be honest about my emotions instead of bottling everything up! This is when our teacher provided me with this pinwheel. He told me something I didn't know before: there were two ways to cope with emotions: positive and negative.

He talked to me about negative coping methods and how I could avoid all of them, focusing on the positive methods. That day, I also told my mom about what the teacher had told me, and my mom helped me look for more positive coping methods after dinner that day.

This is a comprehensive pinwheel of negative and positive coping methods that you can use to turn your negative coping methods into positive ones!

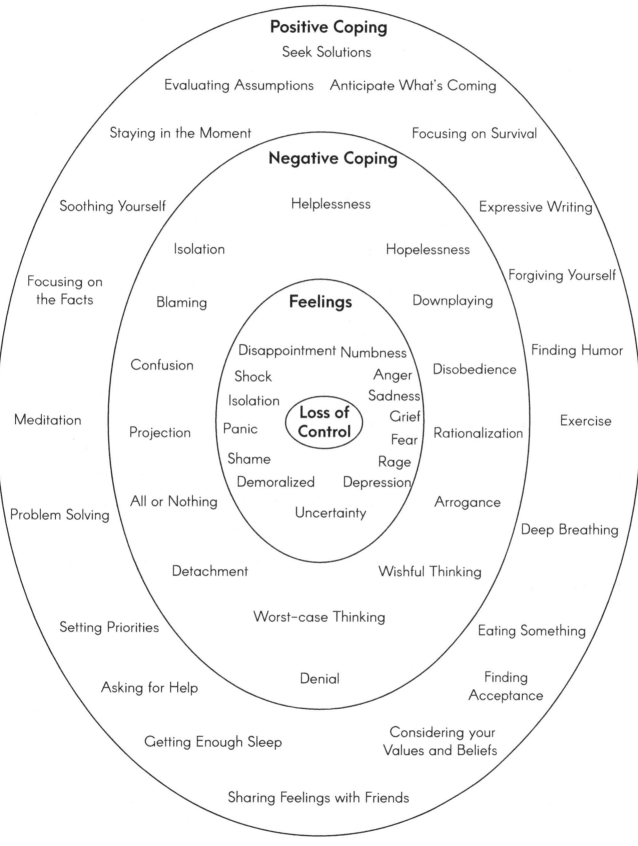

Activity 14

THE ABCS

Hi again, friends; how has your self-regulation journey been so far? I hope you're having as much fun learning self-regulation as I am guiding you about all the coping methods! I admit that learning to regulate and control your emotions can be a tough job! When the exercises and activities start to get tough, I like to take a little break and sing the A.B.C.s of self-regulation. You, too, can sing this song when you need to remind yourself of the self-regulation A.B.C.s. Sing this to the tone of the F.U.N. song by Spongebob; try to get your teachers and friends join in on the fun, too!

A

A is for Asking help from an Adult

B

B is for Bounce a Ball

C

C is for listening to Calming sounds

D

D is for Deep breaths

E

E is for naming your Emotions

F

F is for spending some time with Friends

G

G is for spending some time in a Garden

H

H is for keeping your Hands to yourself

I

I is for Imagining being in a happy place

J

J is for doing star Jumps

K

K is for Kicking a ball

L

L is for something that makes you Laugh

M

M is for listening to Music

N

N is for counting Numbers back and forth

O

O is for going Outside for some fresh air

P

P is for Painting a Picture

Q

Q is for going to a Quiet place

R

R is for Running as fast as you can

S

S is for Stretches

T

T is for Taking yourself away from the situation

U

U is for drawing yourself away from what Upsets you

V

V is for getting Vocal and addressing your feelings

W

W is for drinking Water

X

X is for taking deep Exhales and inhales

Y

Y is for trying easy Yoga

Z

Z is for Zoning out

MY CHECK-IN TOOLKIT

After going through the ABCs calm down song, you will have fun with this given activity.

My check-in toolkit is an interactive activity involving arts and crafts. I often do this activity with the help of my dog, Max! It may seem strange to some people, but it's true! He helps me by bringing me colors from my desk or calling my mom when I need her, but I'm too busy with my activity to go call her myself!

The check-in toolkit is an activity that helped me develop many effective methods to deal with my stress and anxious feelings. You can also create personalized coping methods, too! Here is what you will need:

- Scissors
- Glue
- Some colored A4 size pages

I will list the emotions, and you must think of effective coping methods. Then, the fun part starts: take your arts and crafts supplies, create pictures for these coping methods, and paste them under the emotion!

When I feel sad, I can...

When I
feel angry,
I can...

When I feel scared, I can...

When I feel nervous, I can...

Activity 16

ROLL YOUR EMOTIONS BOARD GAME

The last activity in this section is a fun game you can play with your friends and family. After going through the strategies and activities, try this board game. The instructions are simple: The first one to reach 'Finish' wins!

1 Start

2

3

4

5 Yippee, you feel great! Move to 8

6

7

8

9 You're feeling ill, miss 2 turns

10

11

12 You're feeling angry, go back to 9

13

14

15

16 You're feeling scared, miss 2 turns

17

18 You're pulling a silly face, miss a turn

19

20

21 You're feeling anxious, move carefully to 24

22

23 You're happy, dance to 25

24

25

26

27

28
You're feeling sad and need someone to talk to, go back to 25

29

30

31

32

33
You're happy doing school work, roll an even number and move to 50

34

35

36
You're angry, stomp back to 34

37

38

39

40
You've been silly in class, go back to 37

41
You're worried and need a timeout. Miss a turn

42

43

44

45
You're being tickled, run to 49!

46

47

48
You're feeling nervous, miss a turn

49

50

51

52

53

You have to go to the principal's office, miss a turn

54

55

56
You're frustrated. If you roll an odd number, go back to 35

57

58

59
You fell over! Fall to 60

60

61

62
You're bored. If you roll an odd number, move back to 58

63

64

65

66

67
You're excited! Leap to 70

68

69

70
You're going on a car ride, move to 73

71
You have lots of energy, run to 74

72

73

74

75
You're sleepy, miss a turn

76

77

78
Your school work is excellent, have an extra turn

79

80

81
You're listening to your favorite song, dance to 84

82

83
You have to go to the dentist, go back to 79

84

85

86

87

88

89

90

91

92

93
You've got a cold, miss a turn

94

95
You're sad because you accidentally broke your toy. Roll an even number and move to 97

96

97

98

99

100

Finish

Note to Parents

Sit with your child and play this board game. Have some fun, and make sure that your child can properly de-stress and regulate their calm emotions after going through the previous activities.

Badge Acquired!

Well done! You have finally gone through the entire section and started your progress towards learning self-regulation by coping with intense emotions! After completing all the exercises above, you have completed your first step in this journey; I'm proud to call you my friends!

Here's a badge for completing this section!

Creating Emotional Awareness

Emotional awareness has been a challenge for me to grasp in my journey to self-regulate. It is still the one aspect that I struggle the most with because I can never tell how certain things are supposed to make me feel in different situations! My dad often helps me understand my emotions, and he has even trained our dog Max to physically get in my way and stop me from reacting in big ways when I start to feel frustrated and can't identify why a situation is making me frustrated.

THIS MAKES ME FEEL

My Friends! If you also find it difficult to identify your emotions, let me tell you that it is crucial to identify when certain situations make you feel big and explosive emotions. Here is how you can do that. I will list some emotions below, and you can use the given boxes to list what makes you feel that particular emotion.

Think about the last 2 weeks. Has there been a situation where one of these intense emotions arose in you? Then, list the solutions you used to deal with those emotions and if they were the correct solutions. If not, what alternatives could you have used?

SITUATIONS THAT MAKE ME FEEL

Happy

When I felt _____, I _____

_____

Was this the correct solution?

_____

If not, what could I have done instead?

_____

Sad

When I felt _____, I _____

_____

Was this the correct solution?

_____

If not, what could I have done instead?

_____

Angry

When I felt _____, I _____

_____

Was this the correct solution?

_____

If not, what could I have done instead?

_____

Loved

When I felt _____, I _____

_____

Was this the correct solution?

_____

If not, what could I have done instead?

_____

Bored

When I felt _____, I _____

_____

Was this the correct solution?

_____

If not, what could I have done instead?

_____

Activity 18

WHICH ZONE ARE THEY IN?

Friends, I also like this activity because it's easy, and all I have to do is match the expressions!

When I have trouble understanding other's emotions, I study the expressions of other people and try to guess what they must be feeling! This is a great way to create emotional awareness. Color in the boxes and solve the activity!

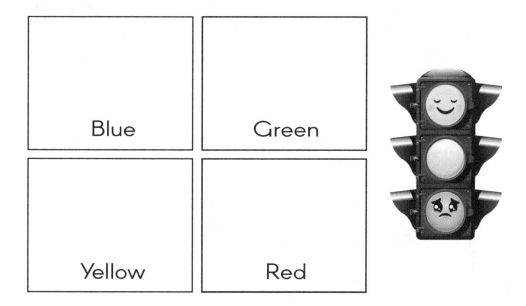

Blue	Green
Yellow	Red

Instructions: Look at the pictures and decide which zone they should be in based on their expressions.

_____ _____ _____

_____ _____ _____

_____ _____ _____

_____ _____

Activity 19

WHICH ZONE ARE THEY IN?

This next activity is based on the previous one. After identifying the zones based on expressions, the next step is easier to practice! Once you have identified the emotions, it will become easier to build emotional awareness yourself!

I have come far in my self-regulation journey, but I still sometimes have problems identifying how I should react in certain situations. This is where I practice this activity, and I often take help from my mom, too! She is there to tell me when my reaction is appropriate and when I should show a different reaction. You can do the same. Color in the boxes and solve the activity!

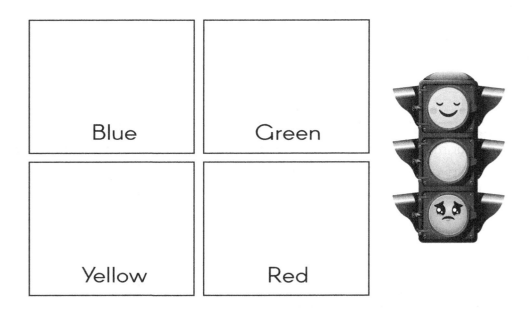

Blue	Green
Yellow	Red

Instructions: Look at the pictures and decide which zone they should be in based on their expressions. Color the cards based on which emotion you would feel in the given scenarios.

Today is your friend's birthday, and you can't find the shirt you were going to wear.	You want to eat ice cream, but your mom says you can't do it before dinner.	You go shopping with your mom, but the store is really crowded.
You have won first place at your school talent show.	Your school trip to the aquarium gets canceled due to bad weather.	The teacher asked you to read out loud in class, but you accidentally mispronounced a word, and everyone laughed.
You want to go out and play with your friends, but your mom says you can't until you clean your room.	You scored 90% on a test you studied hard for.	You had a bad dream last night, and now you're tired due to not being able to sleep properly.
You asked your mom to make your favorite meal, but she said no.	Your dog ate something they weren't supposed to and got sick.	Your dad must travel for work, and you won't see him for 2 weeks.
You wanted to get home quickly from school to watch your favorite cartoon but got stuck in traffic for 45 minutes!	You beat your sister in a game of Uno.	

Activity 20

LEARNING TO SAY SORRY

As a kid who has been practicing self-regulation for a while now, let me tell you this, my friends: learning to say sorry is very difficult. It is often hard to admit when you have made a mistake and even harder to apologize. However, keep this in mind: your unintentional and impulsive reactions can hurt the feelings of those around you, and it's important to show them that you are sorry about how you behaved, so you can work towards rebuilding a strong relationship! Look at some of the ways to say sorry. Draw some more ways that you can also use to say sorry when you make a mistake.

Say, "I am sorry."

Do something nice for the person you have hurt.

Bake a sweet treat for the person you have made upset.

Make an apology card for the person you have made upset.

Spend some quality time with the person you have made upset.

Write an apology letter explaining your feelings and remorse.

Now it's your turn. Use the given page and draw different ways to apologize for your emotional and impulsive reactions!

WHAT ELSE COULD YOU DO TO SAY YOU ARE SORRY?

Draw your ideas!

Badge Acquired!

Well done! You have finally gone through the entire section on creating emotional awareness! After completing all the exercises above, you have completed your second step in this journey; I'm proud to call you my friends!

Here's a badge for completing this section.

Dealing with Impulsive Behavior

Impulsive behavior is when you act quickly without thinking about the consequences. Learning how to stop and think before reacting helps you make better choices, stay calm, and avoid mistakes. In this section, you will explore ways to manage those impulses and stay in control, even in tough situations!

Activity 21

TAKING PERSPECTIVE

My dear friends! Perspective-taking is an exercise that you can use when you are frustrated and need to understand the perspective of the other person. My mom often helps me through this activity when I get too upset over small things around the house or with my friends. It helps me understand the emotions and inner feelings of the people around me, and you can do the same to calm down!

Here is what to do:

Consider the situation! In the given section, I will describe a situation. You can ask your parents for help and try to see the problem from the characters' perspective. Focus on the positive and possible justifications instead of the obvious negative situation. You will see that your feelings about the situation will change when you learn more, which can help you self-regulate better!

Consider the Situation 1:

Lily and Clark were siblings. Their mom told them that she would make spaghetti for dinner. Clark was happy, and he jumped up and down in excitement, but Lily was upset, so she ran to her room and refused to eat dinner.

Why do you think Lily reacted this way? Give your perspective!

_____

_____

Consider the Situation 2:

Ana asked Kelly if she would like to have a sleepover on the weekend, but Kelly said, "No." Ana was hurt and upset, and she wondered if this was because Kelly didn't like her anymore.

Why do you think Kelly said no? Give your perspective!

_____

_____

This next part of the activity is something you can do with your parents! I will list a few things. You and your parents can give your perspectives on the situations and compare the perspectives.

Topic	My perspective	Parent's perspective	Similar or Different?
Mom didn't make the dish you like for dinner.			
Dad didn't buy you the pair of shoes you wanted.			
Your cousins came over when you were in the middle of studying for an important test.			
You couldn't find your favorite jacket in the morning and had to wear a different one to school.			
Your pet took a bite of your dinner when you weren't looking.			

Note to Parents

Sit with your child and talk about different perspectives. Discuss a situation in which both of you had differing perspectives, how the situation was resolved, whether the result was favorable, and what could be done next time to resolve the situation peacefully.

Activity 22

THE PROS AND CONS

Friends, a good way to distract yourself from your rising emotions is to weigh the pros and cons of your reactions! This is a cool trick my English teacher taught me. She always encourages us to think before we make a decision in class, and she encouraged me to do the same when I was having trouble controlling my emotions in class one day.

Apply the pros and cons to your daily life and learn to self-regulate before things get too heavy!

Scenario 1

My pet ruined my school project, and I exploded in a fit of anger.

Pros:
I could vent my feelings.

Cons:
My pet did not understand what they did, and I might have made them scared of me with my meltdown.

Scenario 2

Pros:

Cons:

Scenario 3

Pros:

Cons:

Scenario 4

Pros:

Cons:

Scenario 5

Pros:

Cons:

Note to Parents

Sit with your child and consider the pros and cons of all the situations in the past when they had high emotions; talking things out will help them understand what they could have done differently to self-regulate their emotions.

Activity 23

EMOTIONS RECOGNITION BOARD GAME

Dear friends! This game can be played as a family activity. Gather all your family members and play this board game! The rules are simple: Every time you land on an emotion, talk about a time you felt it in an extreme form, acted impulsively, and what you did to deal with it! You can use this game to distress and learn more about your emotions at the same time.

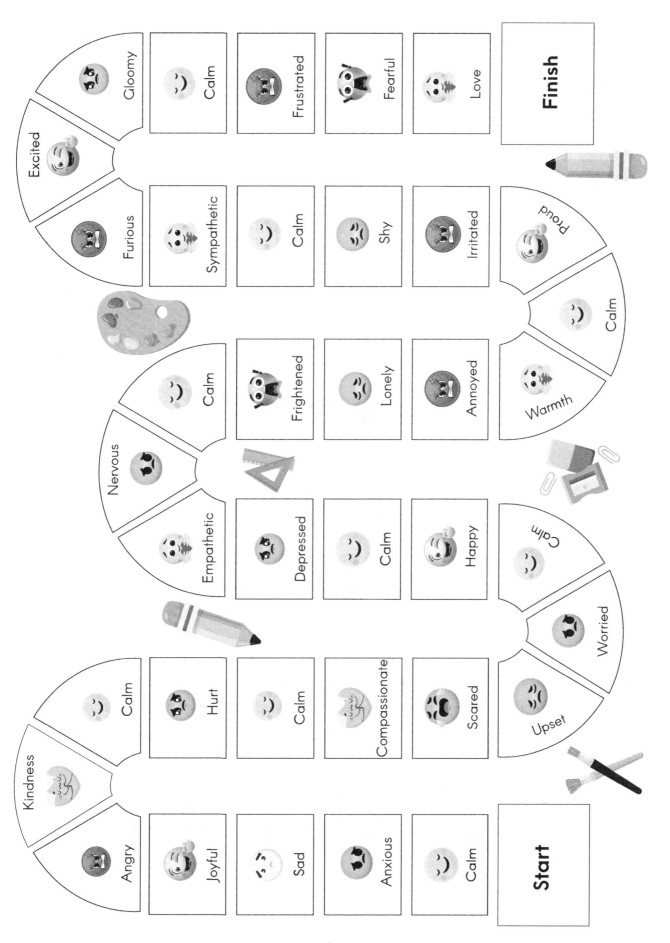

Activity 24

THE SIZE OF MY PROBLEMS

Do you know? When I panic over small things quicker than I should, my dad always tells me that it's because I can't judge the size of my problems. I always overthink small problems, and it causes me to have anxiety and nervousness, resulting in anger fits.

My parents have been helping me learn the size of my problems, and now I can evaluate the size of my problems whenever I feel overwhelmed. Let me tell you all about it, so you can practice the same method to determine the size of your problems!

Take a look at the given problems. Do they sound familiar to you? Can you match them to the appropriate size? Cut out the problems and pin them in the size column.

You and your best friend can't decide what game you should play.

You didn't get time to finish your test before the bell rang.

Your homework is too hard to do on your own.

Your mom won't make your favorite dish for dinner tonight.

Your sibling won't let you play on their computer.

The grocery store is out of the flavored milk you like.

You can't go to a friend's birthday party because your dad came down with a cold and can't drive you there.

You want to eat sweets before dinner, but your mom doesn't allow it.

Someone at school took a bite of your lunch without your permission.

Your friend borrowed your favorite crayon but broke it while they were coloring with it.

Match the problems to the chart given below:

1 TINY	

2 SMALL	

3 MEDIUM	

4 BIG	

5 EMERGENCY	

Note to Parents

Sit with your child and talk about some problems that may seem big but are small. Discuss with them how to judge the size of their problems accurately and which problems warrant big or small reactions.

Badge Acquired!

Well done! You have finally gone through the entire section on dealing with impulsive behavior! After completing all the exercises above, you have completed your third step in this journey; I'm proud to call you my friends!

Here's a badge for completing this section.

Learning to Make Decisions

To make a choice is to be in charge of and taking responsibility for your decisions! In order to live your life in the way you want, you need to think carefully about the choices you make and how they will affect you and the people around you. By using CBT methods to self-regulate, you can learn to make smart choices that turn out well!

THE FEELINGS MONSTER

Use this activity to give emotions to the monsters. How do you think they are feelings? Correctly identifying the emotions can greatly help with your decision making skills!

Use the given box for help, or ask an adult!

Monster Happy Sad

_____
_____
_____
_____

_____
_____
_____
_____

Monster Angry Scared

_____
_____
_____
_____

_____
_____
_____
_____

Monster

Love

Calm   Loving

_____
_____
_____
_____

_____
_____
_____
_____

Note to Parents

Sit with your child and search for more images with different expressions. Variety in emotions can help your child learn faster.

Activity 26

WOULD YOU RATHER

Would You Rather is one of my favorite games! My friends and I love to play it at school, but do you know you can use the same game to regulate your emotions?

I will give you a few scenarios. Choose according to what you think is the right way to react. This is a fun scenario game that can help you develop your self-regulation skills. You can even play this game with friends and family!

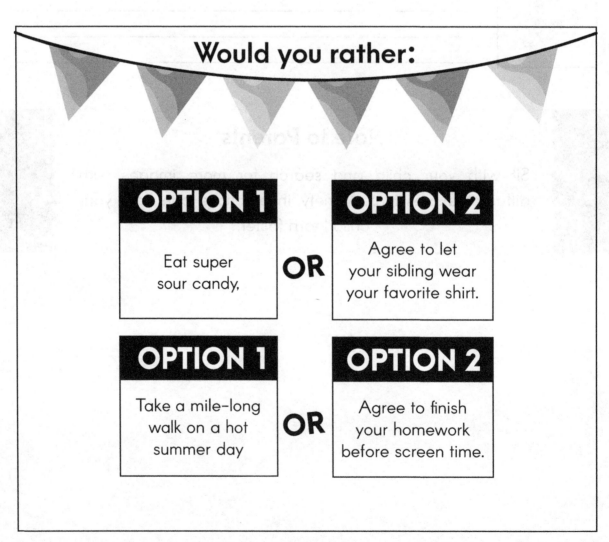

Would you rather:

OPTION 1

Eat super sour candy,

OR

OPTION 2

Agree to let your sibling wear your favorite shirt.

OPTION 1

Take a mile-long walk on a hot summer day

OR

OPTION 2

Agree to finish your homework before screen time.

Would you rather:

OPTION 1
Take an ice-cold bath in winter

OR

OPTION 2
Let one of your family members pick the movie for movie night.

OPTION 1
Eat something super spicy

OR

OPTION 2
Help your mom with the house chores.

OPTION 1
Go without screen time for 1 week

OR

OPTION 2
Practice juggling with your eyes closed.

Note to Parents

Sit with your child and come up with more questions. Incorporate elements of self-regulation and controlling emotions into the game; this will keep things interesting and educational.

Activity 27

A PAN FULL OF COPING

One method I love for coping with my big emotions is to use this pan full of coping activities. Get help from an adult around you, and come up with coping techniques that will help you in tough situations!

Uh oh! The emotions pan is boiling over! Use your coping skills to list difficult situations and the coping skills that help you in these situations!	**Simmer** Good Mood, Happy Thoughts, and Nice Behaviors	**Rolling Boil** Low Mood, Angry Thoughts, and Oops! Behaviors	**Boiling Over** Terrible Mood, Out-of-Control Thoughts and Unsafe Behaviors
My Coping Skills	Goal: Keep the pan simmering	Goal: Return to simmering	Goal: Return to simmering
How Adults Can Help Me	Goal: Maintain the simmering	Goal: Lower the heat and add something to decrease the boiling emotions	Goal: Immediately remove the pan from heat, keep the emotions from boiling over, and call help from the kitchen (adults)

Activity 28

BREATHING TECHNIQUES FOR CALMING DOWN

Friends! Another effective method my parents have taught me to calm down is breathing. I know that breathing techniques may sound boring. They seemed boring to me too at first! This is until my dad taught me this cool game to maintain my breathing. Whenever I feel overwhelmed, I practice these breathing techniques to calm down. They always help me see the best solution in any situation and strengthen my decision making!

You can use the following shapes and trace your finger along the lines while you breathe in and out!

Start Breathing

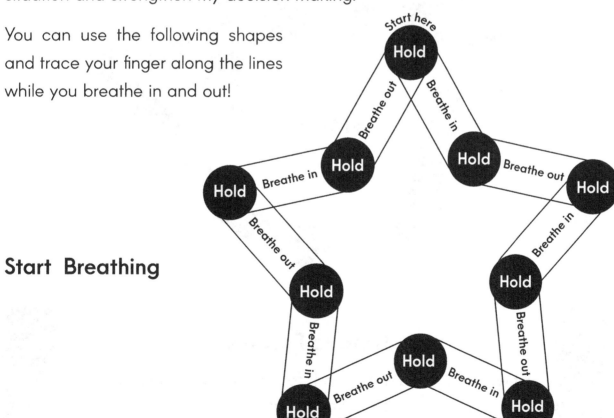

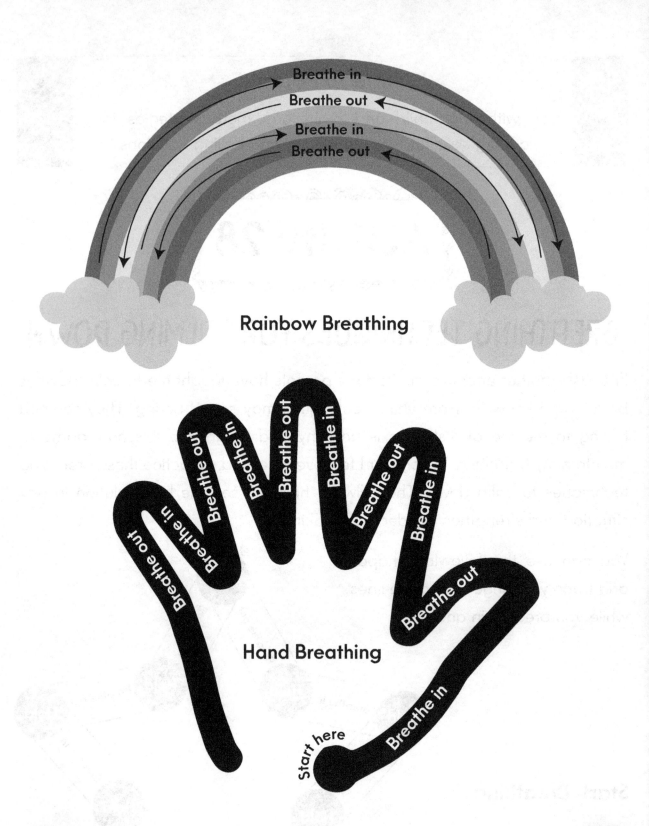

Rainbow Breathing

Hand Breathing

Activity 29

RAIN

One important thing to remember when you are experiencing overwhelming emotions is that you are not defined by that emotion. My mom has helped me understand that it's okay to feel overwhelmed by your emotions, but after the emotion has passed, you must also repent of any mean things you said and did. Little by little, you will start to improve your self-regulation!

You can easily do this with the RAIN activity. Which can help you distress and bring your attention back to the process of self-regulation.

R A I N

R Recognize what is happening and the emotions taking place in your body.

A Allow the feeling to pass through your body like the rain.

I Investigate your inner feelings; how does this feel in your body?

N Natural awareness is important. You are not this emotion. It will go away, and you will feel better

Note to Parents

Sit with your child and discuss when they feel guilty after a meltdown. Children often have trouble letting go of guilt, and it's important to let them know that their flared emotions do not define them. Help them decide which emotions are important enough for them to feel guilty about and apologize for, and which ones to let go of.

Activity 30

STORY CHOICES

These self-regulation stories are part of my personal collection of self-regulation exercises, partly because I love to read stories and partly because I enjoy learning new self-regulation techniques! These stories will help you decide which decisions should be made in tough situations and how you can deal with your emotions while making these decisions.

You need to read the stories and give answers according to what you think is right!

Story 1:
You are at school, and one of your friends falls and scraps their knee.

Your Answer:

_____

_____

_____

Story 2:

Your pet suddenly passed away, and you're really sad. You don't want to go to school but have a really important test.

Your Answer:

_____

_____

_____

Story 3:

Your soccer team lost a really important match which you practiced hard for.

Your Answer:

_____

_____

_____

Note to Parents

Sit with your child and brainstorm more stories to teach them the importance of decision making in regulating emotions through stories.

Badge Acquired!

Well done! You have finally gone through the entire section and taken the step towards decision making to regulate your emotions! After completing all the exercises above, you have completed your fourth step in this journey; I'm proud to call you my friends!

Here's a badge for completing this section

Improving the Ability to Manage Behavior

Friends! Self-regulation is a skill that takes many attempts to learn and perfect. In my case, I have discovered that anger is one of those emotions I find the hardest to self-regulate!

My body reacts so strongly that I'm often unable to identify the point where small emotions turn into big ones. If you also experience such feelings, I have a fun coloring activity to help you!

WHEN I FEEL MAD

This exercise can help you manage your behavior, emotions, and feelings when you feel mad.

Note to Parents

Sit with your child and brainstorm more coping methods for managing their anger. Let them know that feeling the emotion itself is not wrong; however, it's also essential to learn how to control it and behave in such situation.

WHEN I FEEL SAD

Just like the activity given above, this one also focuses on managing strong feelings, such as sadness or anxiety, that can get out of control easily and are harder to manage on your own! Feeling sad is not a good feeling, and I don't like it when I start to feel down, so I often use this activity to cheer myself up!

Take deep, calming breaths

Hold a pillow or stuffed animal

Eat something sweet

Take a nap

Listen to calming music

Watch a funny movie

Spend some time with a pet

Vocalize your feelings

Let your feelings out by drawing/painting

Activity 33

COPE-CAKE

Cope-cake is a delicious coping activity that can help you manage your impulsive behavior. This activity teaches you which skills are healthy coping behaviors and which skills are unhealthy and should be avoided.

You can even do this activity with your parents. Whenever I practice cope-cake, my mom and I bake cupcakes afterwards and she even sneaks me a cupcake before dinner!

Here is what you need to know about this activity:

WHAT IS A COPE-CAKE?

It is the way you can cope with any situation. There are many methods to cope with big and impulsive feelings when they become overwhelming; however, it is important to identify whether the coping skills you're using are healthy or not.

Some healthy coping skills include taking deep breaths or going on calming walks. Some unhealthy coping skills can be yelling, hitting, and hurting others or yourself.

When you start to feel overwhelmed by big emotions, you can use healthy coping skills to calm yourself and then return to the activity you were doing before you became upset or sad.

So go ahead and list the coping methods that suit you best in these six cupcake flavors! You can also color them in to make the activity more fun!

A DOZEN CUPCAKE FLAVORS

COPE-CAKE RECIPE

In the given worksheet, write down the ingredients (coping methods, such as breathing techniques) and their directions (e.g., the steps to breathing techniques.)

INGREDIENTS:

_____

_____

_____

_____

DIRECTIONS:

_____

_____

_____

_____

COPE-CAKE MATCHING:

Match the healthy and unhealthy coping skills, and color the cupcakes!

Yelling and screaming

Counting to 10

Stretching

Telling someone what you need

Kicking and hitting

Getting a glass of water

Breaking your toy

Note to Parents

Sit with your child and solve the cope-cake activity. Help them understand healthy vs unhealthy coping habits and skills.

Activity 34

MY CALM DOWN SONGS

One of my favorite coping methods to deal with strong emotions is singing! Nursery rhymes have always been fun songs I enjoy at any time, so using them as a coping skill for my strong emotions is even more effective! If catchy songs and rhymes can help you calm down, use these songs whenever you need to be calm!

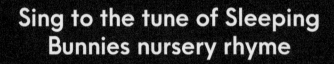

Sing to the tune of Sleeping Bunnies nursery rhyme

Blue Area

Frogs are in the blue spot
Sitting very very still,
They could be sitting still
Feeling really sad
They're so still
Are they ill?
Still little froggies
Hop, hop, hop,
Hop, hop, hop,
Hop, hop, hop.
Feel a lot better
Hop, hop, hop,
Hop, hop, hop.

Still little froggies
Hop, hop, hop,
Hop, hop, hop,
Hop, hop, hop.
Feel a lot better
Hop, hop, hop,
Hop, hop, hop.

Sing to the tune of Sleeping Bunnies nursery rhyme

Green Area

Dogs are in the green place
Alert and ready to go,
Looking happy, calm
And ready to listen,
They're so calm
Happy now
Happy calm doggies,
Woof, woof, woof,
Woof, woof, woof,
Woof, woof, woof.
Feeling just right now
Woof, woof, woof,
Woof, woof, woof.

Happy calm doggies,
Woof, woof, woof,
Woof, woof, woof,
Woof, woof, woof.
Feeling just right now
Woof, woof, woof,
Woof, woof, woof.

Sing to the tune of Sleeping Bunnies nursery rhyme

Yellow Area

Cats are in the yellow space
Silly leaping up and down,
They are so excited
Silly silly cats
Crazy cats
Silly cats
Wiggly wiggly cat,
Meow, meow, meow,
Meow, meow, meow,
Meow, meow, meow.
Feeling silly now,
Meow, meow, meow,
Meow, meow, meow.

Wiggly wiggly cat,
Meow, meow, meow,
Meow, meow, meow,
Meow, meow, meow.
Feeling silly now,
Meow, meow, meow,
Meow, meow, meow.

Sing to the tune of Sleeping Bunnies nursery rhyme

Red Area

Lions are in the red site
Angry pacing up and down,
They are so frustrated
Angry angry lions
Cross cross lion
Moody lion
Scared angry lion
Roar, roar, roar,
Roar, roar, roar,
Roar, roar, roar.
Really really cross
Roar, roar, roar,
Roar, roar, roar.

Scared angry lion
Roar, roar, roar,
Roar, roar, roar,
Roar, roar, roar.
Really really cross
Roar, roar, roar,
Roar, roar, roar.

Activity 35

MY CALM DOWN JAR

The calm-down jar is a sensory calm-down activity that can immediately calm the senses by diverting your attention from your intense emotions by distracting you. When I first learned to self-regulate, my dad made me use this sensory jar to calm down, which worked like a charm! You can use the same jar to control your emotions, too!

You will need these things:

A jar or plastic bottle, Glitter, Glitter glue, Gel food coloring, Warm water

Method:

1. Add half of the warm water inside the jar until it is filled approximately 1/3.

2. Take ½ of the remaining warm water and add the glitter glue. Mix until both ingredients are combined.

3. Add in a few drops of the gel food coloring.

4. Add in the glitter! You can use the big, chunky kind or the fine powder type!

5. Add the leftover warm water, close the lid, and shake, shake, shake!

6. Use this glittery water to distract yourself whenever a strong emotion arises.

Activity 36

THE ZONES OF REGULATION

Hi friends! The Zones of Regulation is an activity that can help you identify your immediate reaction in situations that may make you have big emotions. Then, you will learn what needs to be done to control your impulses so you can learn to self-regulate better!

Green Zone

Happy	Calm	Okay

Content   Focused

Ready to Learn

Blue Zone

Sad	Tired	Sick

Slow Moving   Bored

Need to Rest

Yellow Zone

Frustrated   Worried

Silly   Excited   Hyper

Loss of Some Control

Red Zone

Angry   Loud   Mean

Yelling   Hitting   Terrified

Out of Control

GREEN ZONE

How I Look or Act

I sit up straight.
I see and hear everything clearly.
I smile and respond politely.

Needed Action

Keep it up.
You are doing great.

BLUE ZONE

I slouch and sigh.
I yawn or rub my eyes.
I move slowly.
I have a sad face or cry.

Pay attention more.
Be energized.
Seek comfort.

YELLOW ZONE

How I Look or Act

I squirm and fidget in my seat.
I roll my eyes and furrow my brows.
I cross my arms.

Needed Action

Take a break.
Do a calming activity.
Ask for help.

RED ZONE

I scream or yell.
I hit or kick.
I lose control.
I stomp my feet.
I cry.

Get help from a grown up.
Using calming strategies.

Given below are some things you may do when you are in a specific zone.
Read them carefully and color them based on the zone you think they belong to.

I can play and enjoy the outdoors. I can read and study. I can help a friend. I can list down why I feel good to help cheer me up when I'm not okay.	I can get a drink of water. I can sit up straight. I can take a short walk. I can tell someone how I feel.	I can stop whatever I am doing. I can step back and think. I can ask for a break. I can ask for help.	I can close my eyes and count to 20. I can take deep breaths. I can think of a place where I feel safe. I can write, talk, or draw about what I feel.

126

Badge Acquired!

Well done! You have finally gone through the entire section of the "Improving the Ability to Manage Behavior" step! After completing all the exercises above, you have completed your fifth step in this journey; I'm proud to call you my friends!

Here's a badge for completing this section

Avoiding Difficult Emotions

Hello friends! You have made it to the final section of this book! After the long journey, I'm happy and proud to see you at this final step! Let's kick off this section and finally work towards completing this journey we began together!

HOW BIG IS MY PROBLEM

How Big Is My Problem is a simple activity that can help you identify the size of your problems! Look at the chart. Study the size of the problems. Then, look at the given statements and put stickers next to them based on your understanding of the size of the problem. You can purchase the stickers from any stationary shop near you!

HOW BIG IS MY PROBLEM

TINY

Tiny problems can be easily fixed, so stay calm and don't panic.

Example: Losing a pencil.

SMALL

Small problems can easily be fixed without the help of adults, and they usually last less than a day.

Example: Forgetting to bring your homework to school.

MEDIUM

Medium problems might need adult help and may hurt other people's feelings, but they can still be solved.

Example: Someone calls you names at school.

BIG

Big problems need adult supervision. They can't be solved alone and may hurt other people's feelings, last a long time, and be dangerous.

Example: You got lost in the store.

EMERGENCY

Emergencies are very serious problems that require adult intervention. They last a long time, affect several people, and require immediate help.

Example: Something catching on fire.

Now read the given situations and put stickers according to the size of the problem!

You ate your sibling's share of snacks, and now they're upset with you.

Someone at school is bullying you.

You get into a car accident.

You lose your pet in the park.

You forget to do your homework.

A curtain in your room catches on fire.

Your father is an hour late picking you up from school.

Activity 37

EMOTIONS WORD SEARCH

Hi friends! The Emotions Word Search game is an excellent way to talk more openly about your emotions and feelings. Here's how you can play! Search for the emotions in the given word puzzle and talk about a time when you felt each of them and how you learned to regulate them.

Emotions

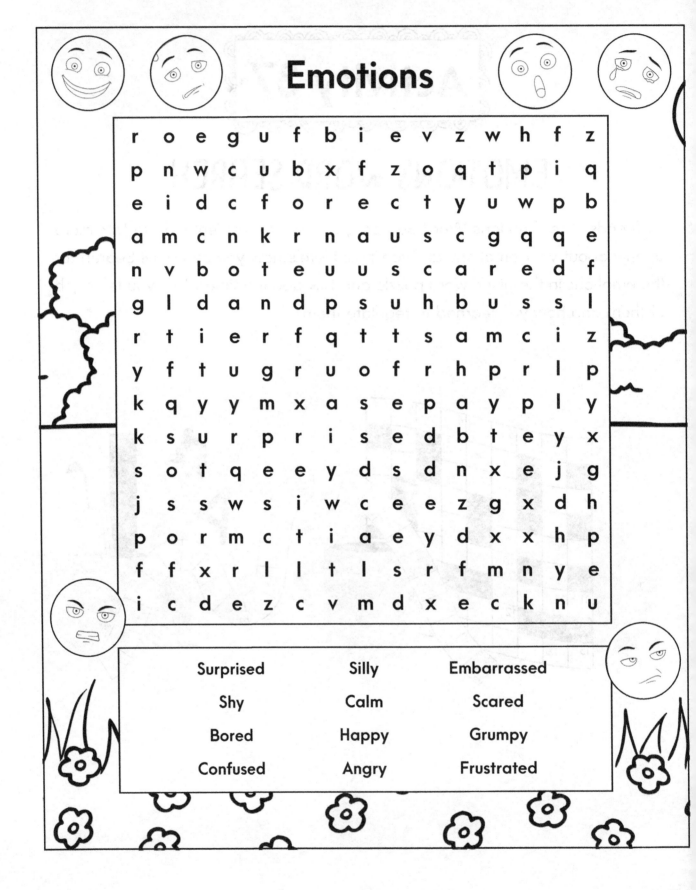

r o e g u f b i e v z w h f z
p n w c u b x f z o q t p i q
e i d c f o r e c t y u w p b
a m c n k r n a u s c g q q e
n v b o t e u u s c a r e d f
g l d a n d p s u h b u s s l
r t i e r f q t t s a m c i z
y f t u g r u o f r h p r l p
k q y y m x a s e p a y p l y
k s u r p r i s e d b t e y x
s o t q e e y d s d n x e j g
j s s w s i w c e e z g x d h
p o r m c t i a e y d x x h p
f f x r l l t l s r f m n y e
i c d e z c v m d x e c k n u

Surprised	Silly	Embarrassed
Shy	Calm	Scared
Bored	Happy	Grumpy
Confused	Angry	Frustrated

Note to Parents

Talk to your child about when they felt these emotions intensely and which strategies helped them calm down.

FINGER LABYRINTH

Hello again! The Finger Labyrinth is an easy and fun calming strategy, and you can even do this without the help of any adult!

Note to Parents

Sit with your child and play the Finger Labyrinth game with them. If they start to feel frustrated with the slow game, gently bring their attention to their rising emotions and suggest calming strategies.

Activity 39

PERSPECTIVE ROLE-PLAY

You can use the given exercise to role-play different scenarios and decide which decisions need to be made if you have difficulty with avoiding emotions. I often practice this activity with my parents, which has helped me improve my avoidance of decisions and difficult emotions.

Here is how you can practice this activity:

1. You need two people for this role play: you and your partner.

2. You will study the scenario and role-play from character A's perspective while your partner role-plays from character B's perspective.

3. After you are done, switch perspectives and discuss character B's feelings while your partner discusses character A's feelings.

Looking at both perspectives; studying the feelings, emotions, and thoughts of both characters can make you realize that there are many factors that make up a situation. There is no definitive answer when it comes to a person's feelings and emotions, which can change under different circumstances.

1. Lost Toy

Character A thinks they lost their toy.

Character B borrowed the toy without asking.

2. Art Class

Character A thinks that Character B's painting looks weird.

Character B explains how the painting has personal meaning to them.

3. Birthday Invitation

Character A wasn't invited to Character B's birthday party.

Character B forgot to give Character A the invitation.

YOU'RE INVITED

Note to Parents

Sit with your child and help them through the role-play scenarios. Discuss the complex emotions they may face in these scenarios and how discussing their feelings honestly can solve most problems that often arise due to miscommunication.

MY CIRCLE OF CONTROL

Hi, My Friends! You have finally made it to the last activity in this section! I'm so happy to finally see you here! With this circle of control activity, your self-regulation journey can finally end!

Let's start the last activity, so you can succeed in this journey! My circle of control is an activity that can put into perspective what you can and can't control. This will make you feel less frustrated when you start to feel angry about a situation you can't control or influence, which will improve your self-regulation skills! Recall any situation in the past when you may have felt overwhelmed, then list what you couldn't control, what you could control and influence.

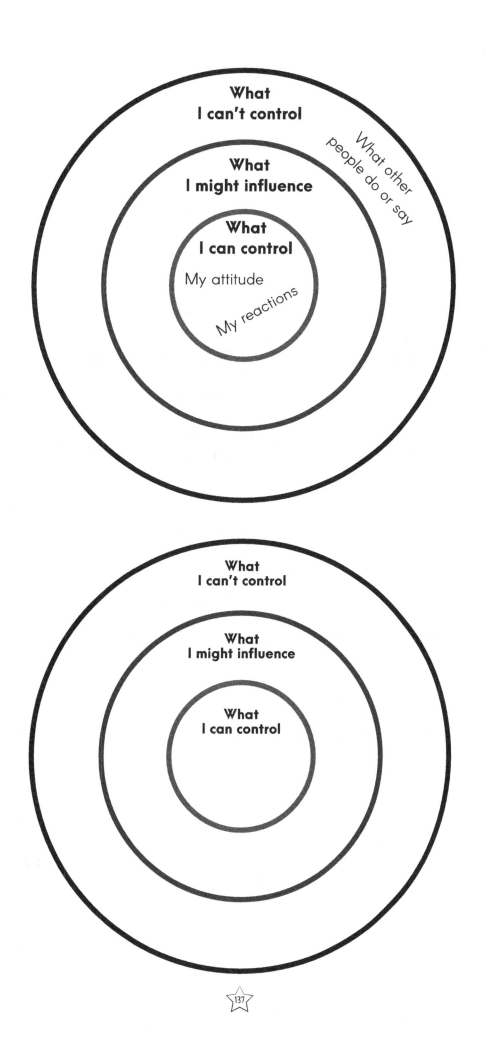

What
I can't control

What other
people do or say

What
I might influence

What
I can control

My attitude

My reactions

What
I can't control

What
I might influence

What
I can control

Note to Parents

Sit with your child and help them remember past events where they lost control of their emotions. Point out all the things that were out of their control at the time. Remind them to let go of their big feelings in similar situations.

Bonus Activity 41

MY STRESS RELIEVING KIT

This is a bonus activity for you, my friends! This stress-relieving kit can become an additional aid for calming down strategies and helping with self-regulation.

You can take a box and fill it with the items that help you calm down. Keep it with you, and use it whenever you feel overwhelmed!

Here are a few examples of what you can keep inside:

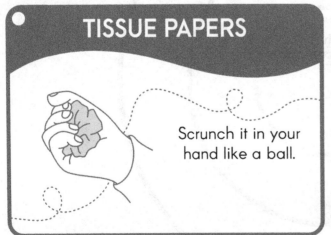

TISSUE PAPERS

Scrunch it in your hand like a ball.

A SMALL BAG OF SAND

Pour it out and draw patterns in it.

PLAY DOUGH

Squish it in your hand when you need to calm down.

BUBBLES

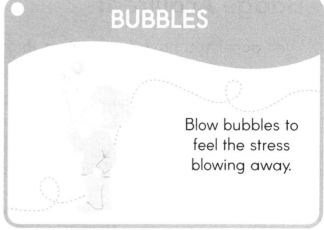

Blow bubbles to feel the stress blowing away.

BUBBLE WRAP

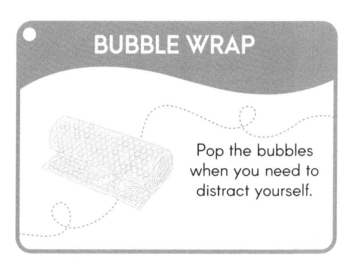

Pop the bubbles when you need to distract yourself.

Note to Parents

Sit with your child and come up with more stress-relieving kit items that can be fun at the same time!

Badge Acquired!

Well done! You have finally gone through the entire section and finished your progress towards learning self-regulation! After completing all the exercises above, you have completed your seventh and final step in this journey; I'm proud to call you my friends!

Here's a badge for completing this section!

RATE YOUR DAY

After the long list of exercises, you have gone through, I bet you're feeling a little bit exhausted! Well, that's completely fine! Emotions can take up a lot of energy, and it's okay to feel tired after acknowledging the uncomfortable emotions in your body. My mom and dad have taught me a fun activity to keep track of all my emotions throughout the day so I can reflect on how my day was! You can use this activity and do the same! For each day of the week, irrespective of whether you practice any self-regulation activities that day, rate how your day went by coloring the shapes, then sit and talk about all the emotions you felt with your parents. Talk about if they were big emotions or small emotions and how you self-regulated!

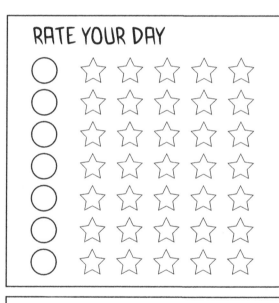

CONCLUSION

My main aim with this book was to provide a comfortable space for kids who want to regulate their emotions. As an adult who suffered from emotional dysregulation in my younger years, I had few resources to better myself. It took tedious research for my parents to find techniques that could help. For today's kids, I want to leave this readily available and accessible activity book that can help them in their time of need.

Sometimes, you will have to mix and match methods that suit you best. I hope you can find the best version of yourself through "Self-Regulation for Kids 8–12."

ABOUT THE AUTHOR

Jessy Torphy is an elementary school teacher living in Queens, New York. She specializes in special education and has helped countless kids develop self-regulation and emotional regulation skills with her over 12 years of experience in this field!

She hopes to reach a broader audience by spreading easy methods and techniques to help children and their parents develop proper emotional regulation with "Self-Regulation for Kids 8-12."

Made in the USA
Monee, IL
27 May 2025

18251958R00079